Mindful Success

Integrate Mindfulness for Peak Performance

Jonas Howard Graham

Table of Contents

The best way to capture moments is to pay attention. This is how we cultivate mindfulness.

Chapter 1. Introduction

Success isn't just about climbing the career ladder, it's about the journey up, too. Our special report, "Mindful Success: Integrate Mindfulness for Peak Performance," explores this very phenomenon that has transformed lives of many successful people across the globe. This engaging guide doesn't just talk theory; it gives you practical tools to integrate mindfulness into your everyday routine – paving your way towards peak performance and holistic success. Unearth the joy of the 'here and now,' and see how it boosts your productivity, enhances your focus, and elicits a sense of inner peace – all fundamental ingredients for success. So get ready to embark on an exhilarating journey of self-discovery and harnessing the power of the present moment for exceptional success. Yes, with our special report, success isn't just achievable—it's enjoyable.

Chapter 2. Unfolding Mindfulness: An Introduction

Mindfulness is a concept deeply rooted in age-old practices and philosophies. Deriving its origins from Buddhist traditions, it speaks to a state of being fully engaged and in tune with the happenings of one's present moment. To be mindful is to be aware, without judgment or bias, of what is taking place within and around us, invoking a sense of profound connection to life in real-time. This chapter aims to unravel the complexities and nuances associated with mindfulness, breaking it down to its core components, such that its essence can be comprehended and embodied.

2.1. Origins and Conceptual Understanding

Mindfulness, as a term, emanated from the Pali word 'sati,' which is often translated to mean 'awareness,' 'attention,' or 'memory.' These translations, while encapsulating the term's meaning, do not fully express its breadth. Essentially, mindfulness encompasses a sense of acute awareness, an in-depth understanding of the immediate, and an unbiased appraisal of the present.

Historically, the practice of mindfulness was central to Buddhist teaching, forming an integral part of the Eightfold Path to enlightenment and liberation. However, the shift of this practice into mainstream realms was spearheaded by Jon Kabat-Zinn, an American professor emeritus of medicine, who established the Mindfulness-Based Stress Reduction (MBSR) program at the University of Massachusetts Medical School in 1979. He put forth a secular definition of mindfulness as the act of "paying attention in a particular way: on purpose, in the present moment, and nonjudgmentally." This opened up the practice to those outside the

Buddhist faith, promoting it as a means to navigate, negotiate, and understand the tribulations of human life.

To dive deeper, let's dissect the definition proposed by Kabat-Zinn. Firstly, to pay attention 'on purpose' signifies the need for a deliberate intention when practicing mindfulness. It involves consciously directing attention to a chosen object. Secondly, mindfulness calls for a focus 'in the present moment.' This highlights the importance of transcending preoccupations with the past or future, and instilling a keen awareness on the occurrences of the 'here and now.' Finally, it mandates an approach 'nonjudgmentally,' recommending an acceptance and recognition of each event, thought, or emotion without evaluating it as right or wrong, good or bad. And thus, mindfulness calls for an unerring and unbiased attention to the orchestration of life, in its raw and unprocessed form.

2.2. The Benefits of Mindfulness: An Empirical Overview

There is a growing body of research attesting to the benefits of the practice of mindfulness, cutting across various domains of life. A meta-analysis of research efforts by Gotink et al. (2015) highlighted several areas where mindfulness showed significant impact, including physical health, mental health, and cognition.

Physically, mindfulness has been observed to contribute to improved cardiovascular health, improved immune response, and amelioration of chronic pain. In terms of mental health, the practice has been linked with a reduction in symptoms related to anxiety, depression and sleep disorders. Cognitive benefits include enhanced attention, improved memory, and greater cognitive flexibility.

The extent and diversity of these benefits propound mindfulness as a powerful tool that could potentially augment various aspects of life and foster holistic well-being. Interestingly, the benefits do not cease at a personal level; mindfulness also ushers in a positive ripple effect at an organizational level, with aspects like enhanced workplace productivity and stellar leadership capabilities increasingly becoming associated with this practice.

2.3. The Practice of Mindfulness: Where to Begin

Embracing mindfulness doesn't necessarily mean engaging in lengthy, formal meditations or withdrawing from society to find serenity atop a calm, quiet mountain. Instead, it calls for inculcating certain simple practices into our everyday routine, which could potentially metamorphose our engagement and connection with life.

Recognition and acceptance form the cornerstone of mindfulness. It calls for acknowledging each thought, emotion, and sensation as it appears and accepting it without judgment, regardless of its nature. This invokes a shift from being 'lost in thought' to becoming a watchful observer of one's experiences.

Practice engaging all senses while performing mundane activities like eating or walking, for instance. As you eat, delve into the myriad of sensations that the act of eating evokes like the texture, taste, aroma, or the color of the food. Similarly, as you walk, engage in a conscious awareness of the rhythm of your steps, the feeling of the ground beneath your feet, or the sense of the wind brushing against your skin.

Initiate the practice of formal mindfulness exercises, like mindfulness meditation, to nurture a more focused, consistent approach to mindfulness. Such exercises act as a training ground, building mental muscle for more effortless transitions into mindful states during everyday activities.

Over time, with persistent practice, these acts enable an easy and spontaneous glide into mindful states, fostering an increasing sense of connectivity, richness and depth to the ordinary.

In demystifying and unraveling the concept of mindfulness, this chapter has hopefully kindled a curiosity within you to delve deeper into understanding and integrating mindfulness in your life. Moving forward, the intricacies of establishing a mindful mindset and how it plays a role in paving the pathway to success will be explored. Practicing mindfulness is akin to embarking on an illuminating journey of self-discovery, enabling a significant transformation in the ways we perceive and engage with the world around us.

Chapter 3. Establishing the Mindful Mindset: Harnessing Your Brain's Power

As we progress on this extraordinary exploration into mindfulness and its role in enabling success, we encounter the reality that this journey originates from one principal source: the human brain. Consequently, to master mindfulness and experience its full range of benefits, we must first seek to comprehend the brain's astonishing capacities and discover how to properly wield its power.

3.1. Understanding the Brain: An Epicenter of Power

Occupying center stage in our journey towards establishing a mindful mindset is the human brain—a complex, multidimensional macrocosm that controls our thoughts, feelings, and actions. Essentially, it is the architect of our reality. Hence, understanding how our brain functions is crucial in harnessing its power for our benefit.

Neuroscience, the study of the nervous system and the brain, offers profound insights about the intricate workings of this essential organ. Among the myriad revelations unveiled by neuroscience, one stands out as critical for our pursuit—neuroplasticity. This principle refers to the brain's ability to change and adapt as a result of experiences and learned behaviors. This dynamic property is at the heart of our ability to acquire new skills, process new information, adapt to changes, and even recover from brain injuries.

3.2. The Power of Neuroplasticity: Shaping Your Mind

The understanding of neuroplasticity becomes especially pertinent when considering the cultivation of mindfulness. As a skill, mindfulness can be progressively developed and firmly entrenched in our daily life through consistent practice, essentially rewiring our brain structures for our advantage. The process of nurturing mindfulness rides on the back of neuroplasticity—it is how repeated mindfulness exercises shape the neural pathways leading to long-term changes in cognitive and emotional functions.

3.3. Mindful Brain: A Biochemical Perspective

At the biochemical level, practicing mindfulness significantly influences key neurotransmitters within the brain—such as serotonin, dopamine, and norepinephrine—which are directly associated with mood regulation, motivation, attention, and alertness. Regular practice of mindfulness also improves the functioning of the prefrontal cortex—the brain's executive control center— thereby enhancing decision-making, problem-solving, and focus.

In essence, your daily practice of mindfulness not only changes the physical structure of your brain by strengthening certain neural connections, but it also influences your brain chemistry, thereby affecting your feelings, moods, and overall mental state.

3.4. The Brain-Mind-Body Axis: Integrating Mindfulness

To effectively harness the power of the brain for mindfulness, it's essential to comprehend the neurological axis that links the brain, mind, and body. This triune system underlies our mental processes, emotions, and actions. Understanding this nexus allows us to see how mindfulness can influence our responses and reactions to external stimuli.

By consciously directing focus and awareness to our present experiences—we learn to respond rather than react, enhancing our emotional regulation and reducing stress. The cumulative result? Enhanced well-being, improved productivity, and the creation of a sustainable pathway to success.

3.5. Practical Applications: Harnessing Your Brain's Power

Now equipped with the fundamental knowledge of how our brain operates and the role of neuroplasticity, we are ready to use these insights to their maximum advantage. But how?

Firstly, it's essential to practice mindfulness regularly. This can include mindfulness meditation, where one focuses on a single point of attention (like breath or a sound), or it could mean adopting mindfulness-based strategies during routine activities. For instance, savoring the simplicity of a meal, deeply listening during a conversation, or immersing yourself fully in a task at hand.

Remember, the brain pays attention to what you do repeatedly. If mindfulness is an integral part of your daily life, your brain will adapt accordingly—neuroplasticity at work.

Secondly, make sure to take care of your brain health, as this will enhance your capacity for mindfulness. This includes proper nutrition, sufficient sleep, regular physical activity, and cognitive exercises among other things.

Lastly, don't forget that inconsistency is an impediment to the process of establishing a mindful mindset. Remember that it takes time for the beneficial neuroplastic changes to become hardwired within the brain. Thus, consistency in your mindfulness practices is fundamental to success.

In conclusion, by comprehending the incredible workings of our brain and understanding the concept of neuroplasticity, we can quite literally shape our minds for success. Empowered by this knowledge, we are better equipped to integrate mindful practices within us, transforming not only our personal and professional lives, but also our overall well-being. This chapter, therefore, provides the cornerstone upon which to build and explore the subsequent principles of mindful success.

Chapter 4. Mindful Success: An Interwoven Journey

The construction and comprehension of the journey to success cannot be compartmentalized; it's a multi-layered and intertwined process that begins and ends with the concept of mindfulness. The chapter presents a meticulous exploration of mindfulness as the foundation of true success, alongside delivering critical and applicable strategies for integrating mindfulness into one's route towards accomplishment.

4.1. Unraveling The Complex Fusion of Mindfulness and Success

Many mark success as the culmination of ambitious pursuits and sheer determination. However, this definition barely scratches the surface. Widening our horizons, we encounter a more profound aspect of success: mindfulness. The interweaving of mindfulness and success might seem abstract initially, but it's indeed quite palpable in our lives.

Mindfulness embeds sincerity and depth into our pursuit of success. It enhances focus and unveils hidden dimensions in our journey. It teaches us to cherish the process and accept the outcomes without robust fixations, thereby combating excessive stress and fostering resilience.

4.2. The Spectrum of Mindful Success

Mindful success encompasses more than mere fiscal gains or societal recognition. It's the harmonious amalgamation of personal growth, peace of mind, and professional advancement.

Here, success implies: - Proactively managing high-pressure situations while preserving inner tranquility. - Facilitating sincere professional and personal relationships. - Excavating untapped creativity and innovation. - Triumphing over hindrances and setbacks, transforming them into opportunities.

Each of these definitions embodies a distinctive aspect of success, reflecting the kaleidoscopic nature of mindful success.

4.3. Laying the Groundwork For Mindful Success

Mindful success entails laying a robust foundation where mindfulness acts as our guide and mentor. Preparation is the cornerstone of this process. Here's a linear, step-by-step elucidation of how we can incorporate mindfulness into our groundwork towards success:

1. Identification: The initial stage entails identifying our objectives, as clear goals fuel our drive towards completion. Mindfulness aids in aligning our objectives with our spiritual, mental, and emotional realm.

2. Planning: Once we spot our targets, we proceed to strategize or outline the course towards our goal, with mindfulness leading the way.

3. Execution: This phase involves activating our plan, staying aware of our progress and adaptable to alterations. Here, mindfulness thickens our resolve and resilience.

4. Evaluation: After execution, we evaluate our efforts and the result, using mindfulness to appreciate and learn from the experience regardless of the outcome.

The mindful pursuit of success doesn't merely lie in achievement, but also in relentless learning and relentless self-improvement.

4.4. Pioneering a Path to Personal and Professional Success

Having established the groundwork, we proceed to intertwine mindfulness into our personal and professional voyage. Something as simple as mindful breathing can alleviate undesired stress, enhancing mental clarity and decision-making capacity. Additionally, mindfulness can refine our communications and collaborations, vital aspects of professional success. Simultaneously, it can act as a catalyst for empathy, kindness, and appreciation in our personal lives, symbols of personal success.

4.5. Case Illustrations: Embodying Mindful Success

Engaging with real-life experiences grants us the opportunity to relate and identify patterns to mindful success. We explore narratives of business magnates, sports personalities, artists, and others who attribute their accomplishments to mindfulness. These stories convey the omnipresence and versatility of mindful success, enabling readers to pick cues and shape their unique interwoven journey.

As we conclude this chapter, it is essential to remember that mindful success is an ongoing transit rather than a fixed destination. It's about learning to navigate the voyage with awareness and understanding, reaping personal and professional growth throughout this fascinating journey.

Chapter 5. Cultivating Mindfulness: Techniques and Practices

Whether you're a seasoned professional seeking new challenges or a fresh graduate embarking on your career journey, integrating mindfulness practices into your everyday routine can significantly enhance your performance and overall quality of life. This chapter delves into the various techniques and practices for cultivating mindfulness, taking you step-by-step through methodologies that will help you embrace the present moment fully, and thereby, unlock unprecedented success.

5.1. The Foundations of Mindfulness Practice

The core of mindfulness lies in stillness, presence, and acceptance. Learning how to establish a tranquil, patient mind makes it possible to approach tasks and situations from a place of open-mindedness and flexibility. The following are several key techniques to help cultivate these ringstones of mindfulness:

1. Mindful Breathing: This is the most basic yet naturally powerful technique for developing mindfulness. It involves setting aside dedicated time for focusing your attention on your breath - its rhythm, temperature, depth, and how it moves in and out of your body.

2. Body Scan: Body scanning encourages groundedness and present-moment awareness by guiding you to shift focus through various parts of your body from head to toe, thereby enhancing your connection with physical sensations.

3. Mindful Eating: This is an exercise in experiencing food more completely. It involves noticing the colors, smells, flavors, and textures of your food, as well as the act and sensations of eating itself.

5.2. Developing a Routine Practice

One of the key factors influencing the effectiveness of mindfulness is consistent, routine practice. As you develop greater familiarity with the techniques introduced above, select one or two that resonate most and commit to practicing them daily. As your proficiency grows, your regular sessions will serve as a sturdy anchor for mindfulness, enabling it to seep into all aspects of your life.

Maintaining a mindfulness journal can be significantly beneficial in reaffirming the commitment to practice. The act of regularly recording your experiences, reflections, and moments of insights can concretely track growth and deepen understanding of your mindful journey.

5.3. Mindfulness Through Movement

Mindfulness is not limited to stillness; it can be cultivated through movement as well. Practices such as Yoga, Tai Chi, and mindful walking are intricate forms of mindfulness that highlight the mind-body connection. These methods encourage deliberate, conscious movements, enhancing focus on physical sensations and bringing you closer to the 'here and now.'

5.4. Overcoming Challenges in Practice

Just like any new venture, cultivating mindfulness may come with its share of challenges: distraction, impatience, judgment, or even skepticism. Consider these not as roadblocks, but as age-old habits of the mind that require patient unlearning.

Techniques such as gentle redirection of attention whenever the mind wanders, compassionate self-talk when impatience arises, and reframing judgemental thoughts as simple 'thinking' are key to overcoming these hurdles.

5.5. Taking Mindfulness Beyond Practice

Ultimately, mindfulness is much more than a set of techniques. It is a way of life, a profound commitment to embracing reality as it unfolds, and a conscious choice to anchor oneself in the present.

The above techniques and practices laid out in this chapter provide a robust foundation for cultivating mindfulness. Practice them with commitment and patience, and you'll see a gradual yet profound transformation in your quality of attention, reactivity to stress, and overall productivity – a boon to your journey of unprecedented success.

Remember, success is not just about the destination but also the journey up, and mindfulness practices help make this journey more enriching and rewarding.

In the following chapters, we will delve deeper into how you can effectively integrate these mindfulness practices into your everyday life and how they can contribute to immense benefits, including peak

performance, enhanced productivity, stress management, and overall
well-being.

Chapter 6. Integrating Mindfulness in Everyday Life

In the realm of self-improvement and personal growth, mindfulness has emerged as a powerful tool for fostering a sense of inner tranquility, harnessing focus, and improving overall wellbeing. Having a firm grasp on the concept and benefits of mindfulness is helpful; however, the true magic happens when we seamlessly weave mindfulness strands into our everyday life. We enter a whole new realm of awareness where every moment pulsates with life and vitality. The journey through this chapter will offer insights into the practical ways to integrate mindfulness at every step of your everyday life.

6.1. The Dawn of Mindfulness: Morning Rituals

The mighty sun ascends the sky, ushering in a brand new day. But before the rush of the day sweeps us off our feet, engaging in mindfulness practices helps to anchor our day in tranquility and focus. Start your mornings with mindful stretching and a few moments of meditation. Bring your attention to your senses as you mindfully savor your breakfast, creating an island of calm in the storm of the waking world.

6.2. A Mindful Commute: Finding Peace Amidst Chaos

Our daily commute often serves as a stress-inducing, anxious-filled period. But it can be an advantageous venue for practicing mindfulness. Rather than getting lost in the chaos, utilize this period to engage in mindful listening—attune to the details of different sounds around you. It's about turning a generally frustrating experience into an opportunity for presence and calmness.

6.3. Mindful Working: Navigating a Demanding Day

Amidst the deadlines and demands of a working day, mindfulness can serve as your guide. While engaged in work, take intentional pauses to recalibrate your focus. Periodically checking with your thoughts, and bringing your wandering mind back to the task at hand, helps maintain mental clarity. Another essential aspect of mindful working is embodying mindfulness in communications—listening actively and speaking purposefully forms the crux of Mindful Communication.

6.4. Mindful Eating: Rekindling the Joy of Meals

Often, we are so caught up in the speed of life that we tend to eat our meals mechanically, without savouring the flavours, texture, and aroma. Mindful eating is an art of reconnecting with our meals. When you eat, just eat. Engage your senses fully, appreciate the source of your food, and transform this mundane act into a nourishing, restorative experience.

6.5. Mindful Leisure: Embracing the Art of Doing Nothing

Our modern lifestyle is marked by frantic efforts to fill every moment with some activity or the other. Mindful leisure is about learning to enjoy stillness, power down, and embrace the art of simply being.

6.6. The Twilight of Mindfulness: Unwinding with Awareness

As the hustle of the day slows down, engage with mindful relaxation—revisit your day in retrospect, take inventory of your feelings, and gently let go of the thoughts. A short pre-sleep meditation paves the way for a good night's sleep, invigorating the mind for the following day.

Furthermore, sprinkling your day with mindful moments, such as mindful walking, observing the nature around you, or conscious breathing, can serve to incorporate a more comprehensive mindfulness practice in your life.

Conclusively, integrating mindfulness in everyday life is about much more than sporadic moments of calm. It involves curating a holistic lifestyle that honors the present, encourages non-judgmental awareness, and nurtures mental tranquility. Like many ventures worth pursuing, it requires commitment, consistency, and patience. But the rewards—a more peaceful, focused, and present you—are immeasurable. Thus, embracing mindfulness in our daily life is an untraveled road to experiencing our lives truly, deeply, and extraordinarily.

Chapter 7. Fostering Peak Performance: Mindful Management of Stress and Negative Emotions

The concept of peak performance in any field of human endeavor often hinges on the effective management of stress and negative emotions. By integrating mindfulness techniques, not only can we transmute these potential inhibitors into constructive force, but we can also find an enduring sense of satisfaction, inner tranquility, and heightened creativity. The following sections delve deep into the essence of mindful stress and emotion management and its implications for enhancing performance.

7.1. Integrating Mindfulness to Manage Stress

Chronic stress is a pervasive aspect of modern life. The World Health Organization refers to it as the "health epidemic of the 21st century." Thankfully, mindfulness emerges as an effective antidote to this epidemic, enabling us to navigate our everyday stressors with greater ease and efficacy.

Through approaches such as mindful breathing, observation and awareness, we can confront our stressors head-on rather than evade or succumb to them. By maintaining a state of conscious awareness of our bodily sensations, thoughts, and emotions, we become able to identify signals of stress early, in turn allowing us to intervene with effective coping strategies.

7.2. The Cathartic Power of Mindfulness in Negative Emotion Management

Mood states and emotional experiences are inextricable from our cognitive and physical performance. However, acknowledging negative feelings as they arise and allowing them to move through us demands courage and practice. Here's where mindfulness plays a vital role.

By fostering a non-judgmental awareness of our emotional states, mindfulness encourages us to accept negative emotions consciously. Instead of becoming entangled in these emotions or attempting to suppress them, observing and acknowledging their presence facilitates their organic processing.

7.3. The Symbiosis between Mindfulness and Peak Performance

Traditionally, peak performance has been correlated to perseverance, grit, and innate talent. Today, a growing body of research introduces another variable to the equation - mindfulness. In contexts as varied as professional sports, creative pursuits, and intellectual endeavors, a mindful state of being directly feeds into record-breaking performance.

Mindfulness exercises such as meditation, mindful walking, or yoga, enable us to remain focused, fully present, and relaxed under pressure—key factors that determine peak performance. Moreover, by managing stress and negative emotions efficiently via mindfulness, we free up mental bandwidth, which in turn fuels creativity, problem-solving abilities, and overall productivity.

7.4. Practical Strategies for Mindful Performance

Integrating mindfulness into our performance-enhancing strategies need not be complex. Here are a few simple practices:

1. Start the day with a few minutes of mindfulness meditation. This helps set the tone for the day, promoting calmness and clarity.

2. Routinely take pause throughout the day to check in with your physical state and emotional wellbeing. This enables self-regulation and brings your attention back to the present moment.

3. Prioritize adequate sleep and rest. Relaxation practices like progressive muscle relaxation or the body scan mindfulness exercise can significantly enhance sleep quality.

4. Engage fully in one task at a time. This practice, known as single-tasking, allows for deeper concentration, better quality of work, and a greater sense of satisfaction.

7.5. An Action Plan for Mindful Management of Stress and Negative Emotions

To reap the benefits of mindfulness, it's paramount to create a consistent, personal action plan. The following steps provide a comprehensive guide:

1. Begin by keeping a stress journal. Note down instances when you felt anxious or overwhelmed. Jot down your physical responses, thoughts, emotions, and the methods you used to cope.

2. Identify stress triggers and map your emotional landscape. Regular entries in your stress journal will facilitate patterns detection, hence enabling you to ascertain recurring stressors or

emotional triggers.

3. Develop a personalized mindfulness practice. Choose mindful exercises that resonate with you. Be it breathing exercises, body scan, or mindful eating, consistency is key.

4. Set aside mindfulness breaks throughout the day. Use these breaks to bring your attention back to the present. Check in with your body and mind. Observe your breathing.

5. Unify your action plan with a holistic approach to wellbeing. This includes a balanced diet, regular physical activity, adequate sleep, and social connections.

To conclude, the relationship between stress and performance isn't inherently antagonistic. By introducing mindfulness into our routines, we can navigate our stressors and emotional landscapes more tactfully, thereby fostering peak performance. In the long run, this fosters a serene, balanced psyche, a holistic success far more gratifying and sustaining than any fleeting victory can offer.

Chapter 8. Applying Mindfulness at Work: Enhancing Productivity and Creativity

In the fast-paced, high-pressure environment of the contemporary work landscape, productivity and creativity are key to standing out and achieving success. The integration of mindfulness in the workplace has been recognized as an effective strategy in augmenting these integral aspects. Exploring this vital area, we dive deep into techniques, beneficial effects, and strategies to apply mindfulness at work effectively, enhancing productivity and promoting creativity.

8.1. The Synergy of Mindfulness and Work

To understand how mindfulness affects workplace productivity and creativity, it's imperative first to examine the intersection between mindfulness and work. At its core, mindfulness revolves around attuning one's attention to the present moment non-judgmentally. In the work context, this promotes a state of enhanced focus, clear thinking, and heightened awareness of one's surroundings and actions—ingredients that stimulate productivity and inspire creativity. With aided concentration, employees can carry out tasks more proficiently, lessening errors and boosting output quality. Meanwhile, when employees approach challenges from a place of calm and clarity, creativity naturally blossoms.

8.2. Techniques to Foster Mindfulness at Work

The magical transformation that mindfulness brings in the workplace doesn't happen overnight. It demands consistent practice through various techniques. Here, some basic yet powerful mindfulness practices have been illustrated.

Deep Breathing: Often, work-related stress can be overwhelming. Taking a few moments to close your eyes and focus on your breath can be a game-changer. Attempt to breathe in deeply, hold for a few seconds, and then breathe out slowly. This technique assists in connecting with the present moment and reducing anxiety levels.

Body Scan: A body scan is a great technique for workers who spend long periods sitting. This practice increases awareness of bodily sensations and stress points by mentally scanning through each part of your body. It encourages relaxation and cultivates a deeper understanding of your stress reactions.

Observation Exercises: Observation exercises can involve concentrating on a certain object or phenomenon for a designated time. It could be the sound of rain, the ticking of a clock, or a simple pen on your desk. The goal is to be fully present and attentive in these moments, which can contribute to sharpening focus and enhancing observational skills, subsequently boosting productivity at work.

8.3. Nurturing Creativity through Mindfulness

While commonly touted for its capacity to enhance productivity, mindfulness can be a powerful tool to unlock creativity as well. The ability to think outside the box often requires a rested mind, free from the hustle and bustle of everyday tasks. By enabling you to focus on the task at hand, mindfulness clears away mental clutter, thereby freeing up room for creative ideas to flow.

Mindfulness practices, like taking mindful breaks, the use of creative visualization, or engaging in mindful drawing activities, can open the floodgates to creative potential. They not only stimulate novel thought processes but also help observe details that might otherwise remain unnoticed.

8.4. The Role of Mindful Communication

Communication is absolutely critical in the workplace. Poor communication can lead to misunderstandings, mishaps, and a breakdown in team dynamics. Implementing mindfulness in our communication—known as mindful communication—can help alleviate such issues. By speaking and listening with full attention and without judgement, we can ensure effective exchange of ideas and foster harmonious relationships within the work environment.

8.5. Results of Mindfulness at Workplace

Adopting mindfulness practices at work consistently can lead to several tangible benefits such as reduced stress, enhanced decision-making skills, and improved emotional intelligence. Further, mindfulness increases job satisfaction, promotes work-life balance, and optimally maintains health and well-being, which are essential for resilient functioning at work.

In conclusion, integrating mindfulness at work can significantly augment productivity and unleash creativity—essential fuels to drive workplace success in the long run. With practice and commitment, mindfulness has the potential to profoundly transform your work experience, paving the path towards a more fulfilling and successful career. Whether you're a business leader or an employee, equipping yourself with mindfulness tools can equip you to effectively navigate the ebbs and flows of the modern workplace and ride the wave of success.

Chapter 9. Mindful Leadership: Inspiring Teams and Fostering Workplace Harmony

We enter into a captivating realm of leadership, one that finds inspiration in the unity of teams and cultivates harmony in the workplace. In this bustling world of achievement and success, we often overlook the significance of having a leader who isn't just adept at getting the work done, but also establishes a sustaining rapport with his or her team. We're all too familiar with the traditional authoritarian style of leadership, which can spur productivity, but can also create stress, resentment, and disconnection among team members. It's time to unfurl the principles of mindful leadership as a solution to these issues, focusing on creating an atmosphere of respect, openness, and mutual growth.

9.1. The Vision of the Mindful Leader

Leadership isn't just about overseeing the operation; it's about directing a vision, a vision that manifests itself in the form of teamwork and harmony. A mindful leader, in essence, is an embodiment of this vision. They play a crucial role in fostering an environment conducive to open communication, mutual respect, empathy, and holistic development. Equipped with the practice of mindfulness, these leaders don't just encourage productivity but also ensure that every team member evolves as a person.

Starting the day with a few minutes of mindfulness exercises such as meditation, yoga, or breathing exercises can prime a leader's mind and body for the rigors of the day. Embracing a culture of mindfulness at the workplace can significantly enhance the overall performance of the team and bring about an unprecedented sense of cohesion among the members.

9.2. Essence of Mindful Leadership

The essence of mindful leadership lies in its ability to inspire a sense of inner peace, resilience, and adaptability. By staying mindful, leaders can be present in the moment, steering clear of stress and distractions, and focusing keenly on the task at hand. They channel their undivided attention, energy, and resources towards achieving the collective goal. The tenets of mindfulness also promote a deep sense of empathy in leaders, enabling them to truly understand their team's concerns, celebrate their achievements, and guide them in the face of obstacles.

Leading with mindfulness also helps leaders instill a sense of purpose and meaningfulness in the work the team does. A mindful leader understands that a collective effort towards a shared goal transcends individual ambitions, ultimately leading to a fulfilling and productive work environment.

9.3. Techniques to Foster Mindful Leadership

Establishing mindful leadership doesn't happen overnight. It involves a series of practices that leaders need to integrate into their daily routines. Here is a list of some effective techniques to cultivate mindful leadership:

1. Regular mindfulness meditation: Setting aside a few minutes every day for mindfulness meditation can significantly enhance focus, decision-making, and emotional intelligence.

2. Mindful communication: Effective communication roots itself in present moment awareness. Listening attentively, responding promptly, and maintaining eye contact are all part of mindful communication.

3. Regular self-reflection: Mindful leaders regularly engage in introspection to identify their strengths and areas for improvement. This self-awareness directs their growth, as well as that of their team.

4. Mindful decision-making: This involves considering all options, impacts, and perspectives before arriving at a conclusion. It ensures fair, thoughtful, and logical decision-making.

5. Encourage mindful practices among team members: Leaders can encourage their team members to practice mindfulness techniques such as meditation or deep-breathing exercises. This not only improves individual performance but also promotes team harmony.

9.4. Mindful Leadership – A Catalyst for Workplace Harmony

By fostering empathy, openness, and respect, mindful leadership acts as a catalyst for establishing a harmonious work environment. Such harmony doesn't just translate into increased productivity but also contributes to the overall well-being of the employees. The principles of mindful leadership empower team members to voice their views and ideas without hesitation, accept constructive feedback, resolve conflicts constructively, and proactively contribute to the team's success.

9.5. Leveraging Mindfulness for Intuitive Leadership

A mindful leader, over time, develops an intuition that enables them to make swift decisions and effectively manage the team, even in times of pressure. This intuitive leadership, birthed from mindfulness, fosters an energetic and harmonious workplace.

In conclusion, embracing mindful leadership opens avenues for inspiring teams and fostering workplace harmony. By aiming to be attentive, understanding, and compassionate, a leader not just achieves their goals but creates an environment that celebrates each journey towards those goals. Seize the power of mindfulness, lead with intent, and open up a new paradigm for success—one that exudes peace, productivity, and prosperity.

Chapter 10. Beyond Success: Mindfulness, Health, and Overall Well-being

The exploration of mindfulness as a tool for climbing the ladder of success has been fairly implicit up to now. However, it is paramount to point out that success extends beyond the realms of career achievements, wealth accumulation, and societal recognition. The true measure of success is deciphered from the alignment of one's physical, emotional, and spiritual well-being. This chapter henceforth delves into a deeper understanding of the ripple effect of mindfulness on health and overall well-being.

10.1. The Cogent Connection: Mindfulness and Health

Mindfulness, at its core, revolves around being firmly grounded in the present moment, away from the ebbs and flows of the past regrets and future anxieties. This state of equilibrium has significant implications for physical health. Numerous scientific studies corroborate the correlation between regular mindfulness practice and improvements in the physiological condition.

Practicing mindfulness results in reduced stress responses, ameliorated manifestations of chronic diseases, and enhanced immune function. It primarily works by helping individuals to effectively manage their stress levels, which indirectly mitigates the risk of stress-induced complications such as cardiovascular disorders, insomnia, and gastrointestinal issues. Furthermore, mindfulness elevates the body's resilience against infections and diseases by regulating the immune response and lowering inflammation rates in the body.

10.2. An Undeniable Nexus: Mindfulness and Mental Well-being

Just as mindfulness has a tangible impact on physical health, it is akin to an antidote for the mind. The mind under the influence of mindfulness learns to let go of spiraling thought patterns and instead, builds an admirable concentration aptitude. It can quell the storms of anxiety, depression, and stress, which often are swept under the rug in the pursuit of traditional success.

Those ingrained in the practice of mindfulness often experience decreased levels of anxiety and depression. They enjoy improved cognitive capabilities, marked by enhanced attention and focus abilities. There is a general upswing in the levels of optimism and contentment, which is associated with increased overall life satisfaction. Increased awareness and acceptance of self fosters self-esteem and buffers negative self-criticism.

10.3. Mindful Living: The Establishment of Harmonious Existence

By integrating mindfulness in every moment, individuals can create a balanced and harmonious way of life, attuning to what's truly essential. They turn away from the mindless pursuit of fleeting and impersonal societal definitions of success. Instead, they foster a condition conducive to immersive experiences, from enjoying daily tasks to cherishing relationships.

This intrapersonal harmony extends outwardly, influencing not just individual health and happiness, but also nurturing the health and happiness of interpersonal relationships. Families, friendships, and work relationships all bloom under the mutual understanding and empathy facilitated by mindfulness.

10.4. The Inception of Holistic Well-being

Bringing mindfulness into the fold cultivates a balanced and harmonious internal environment, fostering the seamless coordination of mental, emotional, and physical health. This resultant state of holistic well-being is the ground from which springs forth joy, peace, and vibrancy.

Consequently, people feel more connected to themselves and others, harbor enhanced empathy, possess a heightened sense of self-worth, experience emotional stability, and cultivate an uninhibited flow of creativity. They relish an enriched quality of life and experience a deep-seated success that is profound and deeply personal.

10.5. Case Studies: Testimonies of Transformation

Several real life testimonies stand as proof to the transformative power of mindfulness on health and overall well-being. In an apparent trend, people who have committed to lead an awakened life through mindfulness, profess experiencing a paradigm shift in their perception of success, health, and general well-being.

In conclusion, by integrating mindful living into our daily lives, we can infuse our journey of success with genuine happiness, health, and overall well-being. This approach to success not only ensures peak performance and noteworthy achievements—it rejuvenates life, nurturing contentment and fulfillment from within. Thus, with mindfulness, we discover a definition of success that resonates deeper and sings harmoniously with the rhythm of life itself.

Chapter 11. Case Studies: Real-Life Experiences of Mindful Success

In the landscape of success, real-life experiences play pivotal roles in grounding abstract concepts and practices. This chapter unveils a careful selection and profound examination of various case studies that distinctly showcase the transformative power of mindfulness. Each case aligns with the overarching theme of Mindful Success, vividly illustrating how integrating mindfulness can lead to peak performance in various spheres of life.

11.1. Identifying the Mindful Effect: Sara's Journey

To begin with, we would be remiss not to discuss the story of Sara, a high-powered corporate lawyer battling the daily stress and burnout prevalent in her profession. Although ambition and tenacity propelled her career forward, she found herself increasingly fatigued, tense, and devoid of genuine joy or satisfaction.

Ready for change, she decided to integrate mindfulness into her everyday routine in hopes of finding a healthier equilibrium. She dedicated herself to regular, intentional meditation, actively practiced moment-to-moment awareness, and embraced a mindful view toward her body by implementing a clean, nourishing diet and regular exercise.

The impact was dramatic and multifaceted. Not only did her stress levels decrease and her overall sense of well-being increase, but she also discovered that her professional performance improved significantly. Her focus sharpened, her decision-making skills became more balanced, and relationships with colleagues and clients flourished as her newfound positive energy resonated with those around her. Mindfulness created a domino effect of success in Sara's life, redefining her concept of personal achievement and fulfillment.

11.2. Unleashing Creativity: Pablo's Transformation

Moreover, it's essential to consider the personal transformation of Pablo, a passionate writer who fell into the trap of the feared 'writer's block.' Despite his love for words and stories, he found it increasingly challenging to generate novel ideas or maintain a consistent writing flow, impeding the progress of his well-loved craft.

In a moment of desperation, Pablo turned towards mindfulness, seeking solace in its promise of fostering creativity. He delved into mindfulness-practices such as deep breathing exercises, walking meditations, and visualization. The results were nothing short of awe-inspiring.

These practices helped him regain his innate creativity by granting him access to his mind's creative depths that he wasn't tapping into before. His productivity soared as he began writing with relentless intensity and his works were appreciated more than ever for their profound creativity and insightful narratives. Pablo's case is an inspiring reminder of how mindfulness techniques can uncover dormant creative prowess and stimulate peak performance.

11.3. Uniting Teams and Creating Harmony: The Macrosoft Inc. Experience

Pivoting from individual experiences, it's valuable to witness the practice of mindfulness at a wider, organizational spectrum. Macrosoft Inc., a renowned tech company, incorporated mindfulness training into its company culture after it witnessed deteriorating levels of employee morale and satisfaction linked to stress and work-related burnout.

Macrosoft Inc. began conducting regular mindfulness workshops, promoting flexible work hours, and even designed dedicated 'Mindfulness Zones' within their offices. The results were transformative.

The company saw an upsurge in productivity, higher levels of creativity, better team cooperation, and a significant decrease in employee conflicts. The employees, on the other hand, reported lower stress levels, a better work-life balance, and a general sense of wellness that they associated with the introduction of mindfulness practices at the workplace.

These cases reaffirm the paradigm of Mindful Success and bring to light the multi-dimensional benefits of incorporating mindfulness into various spheres of life. Whether it is an individual aiming to climb the corporate ladder, a creative soul seeking inspiration, or even an organization aiming for overall betterment, mindfulness presents itself as a powerful tool in harnessing peak performance and achieving holistic success.